Marshmallows AND Bikes

Teaching Children (and Adults) Personal Finance

Written and Created by:
BRIAN NELSON FORD

Edited by:
JASON PALMER

Photographed by:
nb-photography.com
AND JEANIE FORD

Illustrated and Designed by:
NICK AND ERIN BAYLESS

Marshmallows and Bikes
Teaching Children (and Adults) Personal Finance

ISBN 978-0-9798854-0-2

PRINTED IN SOUTH KOREA

To My Girls

With Love, Daddy

CONTENTS

ZOE AND EVA ARE BEST FRIENDS. Not only are they best friends — they are sisters as well. They do everything together. They enjoy wrestling with their Daddy and they love to play with their dog.

ONE DAY, THEIR DADDY wanted to play a new game and teach Zoe and Eva something important. Their Daddy said, "We are going to play the marshmallow game." The girls thought the game sounded very exciting.

1   5

ZOE AND EVA LISTENED CLOSELY as their Daddy explained the rules of the game. "OK girls, here is how we play. You get to choose how many marshmallows I will give you." Zoe and Eva looked at each other and smiled because they knew they were going to like this game. Their Daddy continued, "You can have ONE marshmallow right now, OR if you wait one minute you can have FIVE marshmallows instead. So, if you want to choose FIVE marshmallows all you need to do is wait one minute."

ZOE AND EVA WERE BOTH VERY EXCITED. They could not wait to eat a marshmallow so they told their Daddy, "We want ONE marshmallow right now." He nodded and said, "OK, here you go," and he gave them each ONE marshmallow.

AFTER ZOE AND EVA EACH ATE their ONE marshmallow, they noticed the rest of the marshmallows still sitting on the table. Their Daddy raised his eyebrows when he saw that they wanted more. He gently reminded them, "For me to give you FIVE marshmallows you needed to wait one minute — remember?"

ZOE AND EVA TOLD THEIR DADDY they were now ready to wait one minute so they could each eat the FIVE more marshmallows. Their Daddy shook his head and said, "We will play the marshmallow game again tomorrow." Zoe and Eva felt sad that they had chosen to get only ONE marshmallow.

THAT NIGHT, ZOE AND EVA THOUGHT about how they could have had FIVE marshmallows each if they had waited for just one minute.

THE NEXT DAY, THEIR DADDY CALLED them inside to play the marshmallow game again. Zoe and Eva came running with smiles on their faces. Their Daddy explained the rules of the game once more. "OK, I will give you ONE marshmallow right now, OR if you wait one minute I will give you each FIVE marshmallows."

THIS TIME ZOE AND EVA BOTH SAID that they wanted to wait for one minute and get all FIVE marshmallows. Their Daddy said, "OK, here we go," and began looking at his watch very closely.

ZOE AND EVA COULD BARELY STAND IT — they wanted those marshmallows right away! They almost gave up and asked for ONE marshmallow right now, but then they remembered that they wanted all FIVE and decided to keep waiting.

FINALLY, THE MINUTE WAS OVER. Their Daddy looked up at them with a smile and said, "Wow — good job girls, you waited an entire minute! Now I can give you FIVE marshmallows each." Zoe and Eva were so happy — they jumped up and down with joy! They thought those FIVE marshmallows tasted better than any marshmallows they had ever eaten.

SOME TIME WENT BY AND ZOE AND EVA grew a little older
and forgot about the marshmallow game. Then one day while
they were shopping with their Mommy, Zoe and Eva saw two
shiny new bikes at the store.

"MOMMY, MOMMY CAN WE GET THOSE BIKES?" they shouted.
Their Mommy said, "Do you really want bikes?" Zoe and Eva
responded right away, "Oh yes — we really want bikes."

June

SUNDAY	MONDAY	TUESDAY	WEDNESDAY	THURSDAY	FRIDAY	SATURDAY
					1	2
3	4	5	6	7	8	9
10	11	12	13	14	15	16
17	18	19	20	21	22	23
24	25	26	27	28	29	30

"OK, IF YOU REALLY WANT BIKES you can choose to do extra chores around the house and earn money," their Mommy explained. "In about a month, each of you should have enough money to buy a bike." Zoe and Eva felt a little bit sad because they both wanted a bike right then and there.

THAT NIGHT, ZOE AND EVA REMEMBERED the marshmallow
game that they had played with their Daddy. They decided
that choosing to earn money for bikes was kind of like
choosing to wait one minute for five marshmallows. They
felt happy because they knew that if they waited one month
and did extra chores around the house that soon they could
buy their own bikes.

THE NEXT DAY WAS SATURDAY and Zoe and Eva wanted to start earning money for their bikes as soon as they woke up. But first, their Mommy asked if they had done their regular chores. Zoe and Eva knew that they were expected to keep their room clean. So they quickly cleaned their room by picking up all of their toys and making their beds.

AFTER THEY FINISHED their regular chores, Zoe and Eva started working to earn money. They helped clean the house, they dusted, and they even pulled up weeds in their front yard. They worked really hard.

AFTER FINISHING THEIR extra chores the girls found their Daddy. He paid them some money and said, "Now, Zoe and Eva, this is your money — you have earned it. You can buy what you want with your money — but remember, the more money you save the sooner you will be able to buy your bikes."

ZOE AND EVA really wanted bikes so they saved almost all of their money.

ONE DAY WHILE THEY WERE SHOPPING with their Mommy,
Zoe and Eva saw a toy that they wanted. They asked their
Mommy if they could buy it. "Do you have enough
money?" she asked. They quickly responded, "Oh yes, we
have been working hard and have enough money."

THEIR MOMMY TOLD THEM, "Yes, you can choose to buy this toy with your money. But remember, if you buy this toy you will have less money and then it will take longer to get your bikes." Zoe and Eva looked at each other. They knew that they wanted bikes more than they wanted any other toys — so they chose not to buy the toy at the store.

FOR THREE MORE WEEKS, Zoe and Eva did extra chores around the house. Finally, one month had gone by. Zoe and Eva went to their Daddy and exclaimed, "Daddy, we have worked very hard and saved our money for a whole month. Can we go and buy our bikes now?" Their Daddy grinned and said, "You girls have done a very good job — yes, let's go down to the bike store and buy each of you a bike." Zoe and Eva clapped their hands in excitement!

ZOE AND EVA PROUDLY RODE THEIR BIKES all over the neighborhood with big smiles on their faces. They felt even happier because they had earned their bikes all by themselves by working hard and saving their money.

TIPS AND IDEAS FOR PARENTS
Teaching Children Personal Finance

Teaching children to delay gratification is very important. But it is equally important to remember that each life lesson should be taught with love and patience. In addition, lessons need to be age appropriate.

At the age of three, children can begin to understand basic concepts about money. You can show them coins and let them pretend to use money (under parental supervision). You can begin to explain to your children that Mommy and Daddy work to earn money so that they can pay for their food, clothes, toys and home. Make learning about money fun and interesting by connecting it to the things they use every day.

At age three and older, you can begin to get your children in the habit of working. They can be expected to help pick up their toys and keep their rooms tidy and clean. Our children always enjoy singing songs during clean up time. Chores can help instill the virtue of gratitude in children at a young age. When working with your children or talking about your job, speak appreciatively of your home, food, clothes and especially your family. When you are happy about all of the things you have been blessed with and express this gratitude often around your children, they will learn to value the results of working.

At age four, children can begin to understand how and why they should save money. If they are given money or find some, gently encourage them to save it. Make saving fun — after they have saved enough, you can take them down to the bank and let them give their money to the teller. Many banks have children's savings programs that can help make going to the bank with Mommy or Daddy a great experience.

Around age six, your child can begin to receive an allowance. Usually a couple of dollars a week is plenty. Many parents do not give their children an allowance because they believe that children should always work for their money. We teach our children that they are expected to do chores and help around the house because they are a part of our family. These regular chores have nothing to do with money. We give them an allowance that is separate from their expected chores so that they can begin to learn the basics of saving and budgeting. However, we do not want our children to think they can stop doing chores simply because they no longer want or need the money. Everyone in the family has to complete certain chores. If our children would like to earn extra money for something special, we help provide them with additional opportunities to earn money.

Gently teach your children how to budget and save with their allowance. Give them guidance while they are young but remember that children learn best by making their own choices and experiencing the consequences of those choices. When your children overspend and do not have enough money, do not advance them more money. Let them understand by the choices they make that they need to manage their money wisely.

Most of our best teaching moments are not planned. They occur during everyday life. Look for opportunities to teach your children personal finance and remember that your good example is always a child's number one teacher.

Thank you for being a wonderful parent. If you would like more information on how to better manage your money, please visit us at www.MainstayEducation.com

About the Author
Brian Nelson Ford

Brian Ford, Founder and President of MAINSTAY FINANCIAL EDUCATION has a passion for teaching personal finance. He takes great pride in helping people reach their financial goals and achieve their dreams.

Brian's two main reasons for creating MAINSTAY are:

First, there is a flood of information available regarding personal finance. People struggle with where to begin and what to believe. Brian's goal is to bring simplicity and sound principles to financial education.

Second, most people get their financial information from professionals such as insurance agents, financial planners, or mortgage lenders. While many of these individuals are well-intentioned, they often make their money through commissions on the products they sell — creating an inherent conflict of interest.

Brian envisions a financial education company that provides pure and simple advice — advice that he himself follows and shares with his closest friends and family members.

Most people do not have the opportunity to study about relationships and money in school. Yet this is exactly what Brian did with his formal education. He received Bachelors Degrees in Marriage, Family and Human Development as well as in Business.

Further, Brian received a Masters Degree in Personal Finance from the College for Financial Planning — known for educating the nation's top financial advisors.

Through his experience as a financial planner combined with his background in business and education, Brian is uniquely qualified to impact people's lives for good.

We hope you will visit us at www.MainstayEducation.com